S0-BXV-800

Charles County Public Library
www.ccplonline.org

Customs Around the World

BIRTHDAYS
Around the World

by Mary Meinking

PEBBLE
a capstone imprint

Pebble Explore is published by Pebble, an imprint of Capstone.
1710 Roe Crest Drive
North Mankato, Minnesota 56003
www.capstonepub.com

Copyright © 2021 by Capstone. All rights reserved. No part of this publication may be reproduced in whole or in part, or stored in a retrieval system, or transmitted in any form or by any means, electronic, mechanical, photocopying, recording, or otherwise, without written permission of the publisher.

Library of Congress Cataloging-in-Publication Data is available on the Library of Congress website.
ISBN: 978-1-9771-2368-8 (hardcover)
ISBN: 978-1-9771-2668-9 (paperback)
ISBN: 978-1-9771-2405-0 (eBook PDF)

Summary: Happy birthday! Let's celebrate! All around the world people are turning another year older. What are some ways birthdays are celebrated in Asia? Or in South America? Discover the ways people celebrate birthdays in this engaging series that develops kids' understanding of our diverse global community and their place in it.

Image Credits
Alamy: Agencja Fotograficzna Caro, 15, 19, David Kilpatrick, 18, Party people studio, 16; Dreamstime: Kornilovdream, 17; iStockphoto: Image Source, 25; Newscom: CNImaging/Juan Cheng, 20; Shutterstock: Aleksandrs Bondars, Cover, Alp Aksoy, 11, Anant Jadhav, 21, cowardlion, 23, Creative Caliph, 12, MariaKovaleva, 13, Monkey Business Images, 1, 5, Rawpixel.com, 9, Studio Romantic, 28, Vietnam Stock Images, 27, wavebreakmedia, Cover, YAKOBCHUK VIACHESLAV, 7; Wikimedia: M_nunoo, 14

Design Elements
Capstone; Shutterstock: Stawek (map), VLADGRIN

Editorial Credits
Editor: Gena Chester; Designer: Julie Peters; Media Researcher: Jo Miller; Production Specialist: Spencer Rosio

Consultant Credits
Bryan K. Miller, PhD
Research Affiliate of Museum of Anthropological Archaeology
University of Michigan

All internet sites appearing in back matter were available and accurate when this book was sent to press.

Printed in the United States
PO117

TABLE OF CONTENTS

Birthdays Around
the World 4

Birthday Customs 6

Birthday Food 10

A Year Older 16

Special Ages 20

Shared Birthdays............... 26

Map 29

Glossary 30

Read More 31

Internet Sites.............. 31

Index 32

Words in **bold** are in the glossary.

BIRTHDAYS AROUND THE WORLD

We all have birthdays. How do you **celebrate** yours?

There are many birthday **customs**. Groups around the world do certain things for birthdays. Some birthdays get small celebrations. Some are big celebrations. You may have cake on your birthday. Others celebrate with soup.

But one thing is always the same. Birthdays are special.

BIRTHDAY CUSTOMS

Most customs have special meaning. Some customs have been passed down from parent to parent. Others follow **religion**. Many are done just for fun.

In Jamaica, people use flour to celebrate. Friends and family sneak up on the birthday person. They throw flour at the birthday person. It is hot there. The flour sticks to skin. Others see the person covered in flour. They know it's the person's birthday.

Do you believe in luck?
In eastern Canada, parents
rub butter on their birthday
children's noses. They believe
if they do this bad luck can't
catch their children. They
will have good luck for the
next year.

In India, Hindu birthday
children have many customs.
They smear colored rice paste
on their foreheads. And at
parties, the birthday person
feeds cake to each guest.

A Hindu birthday celebration

BIRTHDAY FOOD

What food do you eat on your birthday? Some people eat their favorite foods. Others eat the type of foods their grandparents would have eaten.

Children in Australia have fairy bread on their birthdays. This treat is white bread covered in butter. Then it is topped with candy sprinkles. It is cut into triangles. Children eat it for breakfast.

fairy bread

11

Others have birthday foods without a lot of sugar. Koreans have seaweed soup on their birthdays. They have it for breakfast. Eating the soup shows respect to the mother. This is because she eats it after she has a baby.

Some Russians eat a birthday pie. It can be filled with meat. Or it can be filled with sweet fruits. The pie has the name of the birthday person carved into the crust.

In Ghana, birthday people enjoy oto. This dish is mashed **yams** with onions. It is topped with hard boiled eggs. Oto is served in a big bowl for breakfast. It is eaten by the handful. Oto can be made into patties too. People get their own patty instead of sharing a bowl.

German birthday cakes are like bread. Instead of putting candles in the cake, people put them in wood wreathes. They have one candle for each year of the birthday person.

A YEAR OLDER

How do you count your age on your birthday? People in the U.S. add one candle on their cakes for each year old. They make a wish. They try to blow out all the candles.

In Hungary, a birthday child's ears are tugged. The child gets one tug for each year old. Each tug is a wish for a long life.

In Ireland, friends give birthday bumps. Birthday people let friends hold them by the hands and feet. Friends lift them off the ground. Then friends bump them on the ground for each year old. They do an extra bump for good luck.

Children in Lithuania are lifted on a chair. They are lifted once for each year old. Then they are lifted one more time for luck.

SPECIAL AGES

Some **cultures** celebrate special ages. In China and South Korea, first birthdays are special. Parents lay things around their babies. The babies grab something. This may tell what they will be when they grow up. If they grab a pencil, they may be a writer.

In the U.S., babies get smash cakes for first birthdays. They play with the cake. They use their hands to eat it.

In Japan, a child's third, fifth, and seventh birthdays are special. The Seven Five Three **Festival** is on November 15. Children of those ages dress in their nicest clothes. They go to a **shrine** to give thanks for good health. Then they have a big party at home.

Children in the Netherlands celebrate Crown Years. Those are their 5th, 10th, 15th, 20th, and 21st birthdays. On these years, they get bigger gifts. Their chairs at tables are covered in flowers or balloons.

Children at the Seven
Five Three Festival

Some cultures celebrate growing older. In Mongolia, babies have a hair-cutting **ceremony**. Parents do not cut their baby's hair until he or she is 2–5 years old. After it's cut, parents stop saying their baby. Instead, they call him or her their child.

In Mexico and Latin America, a girl's 15th birthday is special. She celebrates becoming a woman. She wears a pretty dress. The girl puts on high-heeled shoes. The family goes to church. Then they have a huge party. She dances with her father.

A girl celebrates her 15th birthday.

SHARED BIRTHDAYS

Do you know the day you were born? Some people do not celebrate on that day. Some don't keep track of it. They pick their own birthday. Or they celebrate on a **holiday**.

Vietnamese people celebrate their birthdays on Tet. This is Vietnam's New Year. People turn a year older on that day. Tet is Vietnam's biggest holiday.

Vietnamese family celebrating Tet

Some people have two birthdays every year. Most people in Ecuador are named after a **saint**. They get a card on their birthdays. On their saint's day, they have a big party.

MAP

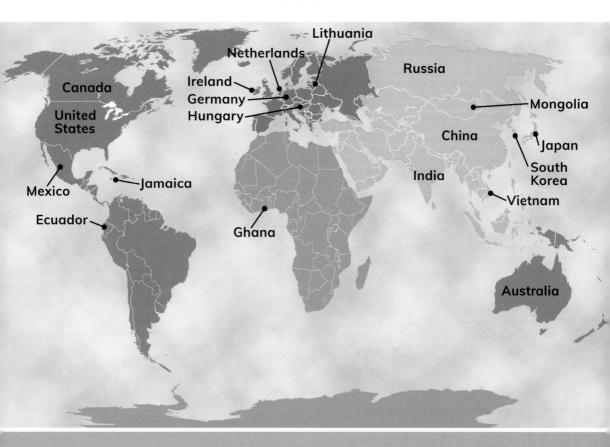

Birthday celebrations are different around the world. How do you celebrate?

GLOSSARY

celebrate (SE-luh-brayt)—to do something fun on a special day

ceremony (SER-uh-mohn-ee)—special actions, words, or music performed to mark an important event

culture (KUHL-chur)—a group of people's beliefs, customs, and way of life

custom (KUHS-tuhm)—the usual way of doing something for a group of people

festival (FES-tuh-vuhl)—a holiday or celebration

holiday (HOL-uh-day)—a special day of celebration

religion (ri-LIJ-uhn)—a set of spiritual beliefs that people follow

saint (SAYNT)—a person who is recognized by the Catholic church for being holy

shrine (SHRINE)—a holy building

yam (YAM)—the root from a vine that grows in the tropics

READ MORE

Gregson, Agatha. *Traditions*. New York: Gareth Stevens Publishing, 2020.

Ian, Nicholas. *Happy Birthday / Feliz Cumpleaños: A Traditional Song in English, Spanish, and American Sign Language*. North Mankato, MN: Capstone Press, 2016.

Klepeis, Alicia Z. *Nigeria*. New York: Cavendish Square, 2017.

INTERNET SITES

Birthday Worksheets
www.education.com/worksheets/birthdays/

Happy Birthday Around the World Game
www.mypartygames.com/happy-birthday-around-world-game/

Nature Cat Birthday Party
www.pbs.org/parents/birthdays/nature-cat-birthday-party

INDEX

Australia, 10

bumps, 18
butter, 8, 10

cakes, 4, 8, 15, 16, 21
Canada, 8
candles, 15, 16
celebrations, 4
ceremonies, 24
China, 20
Crown Years, 22
cultures, 20, 24
customs, 4, 6, 8

ears, 17
Ecuador, 28

fairy bread, 10
festivals, 22
flour, 6

Germany, 15
Ghana, 14
grandparents, 10

holidays, 26
Hungary, 17

India, 8
Ireland, 18

Jamaica, 6
Japan, 22

Latin America, 24
Lithuania, 19

Mexico, 24
Mongolia, 24

Netherlands, 22

oto, 14

parents, 6, 8, 12, 20, 24
pies, 13

religions, 6
rice paste, 8
Russia, 13

saints, 28
shrines, 22
soups, 4, 12
South Korea, 12, 20

Tet, 26

United States, 16, 21

Vietnam, 26